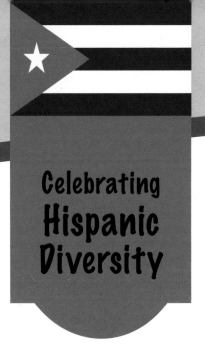

Celebrating
Hispanic
Diversity

THE PEOPLE
AND CULTURE OF
CUBA

Melissa Raé Shofner

PowerKiDS
press.

New York

Published in 2018 by The Rosen Publishing Group, Inc.
29 East 21st Street, New York, NY 10010

First Edition

Editor: Theresa Morlock
Book Design: Rachel Rising

Photo Credits:Cover jcarillet/iStock Unreleased/Getty Images; Cover (background) Gerard Ruiters/ Moment/Getty Images; Cover, p. 1 https://commons.wikimedia.org/wiki/File:Flag_of_Cuba.svg. p. 5 Harvepino/Shutterstock.com; p. 7 Evgenia Bolyukh/Shutterstock.com; p. 9 Everett Historical/ Shutterstock.com; p. 11 gary yim/Shutterstock.com; p. 13 Joe Raedle/Getty Images News/Getty Images; p. 15 Matyas Rehak/Shutterstock.com; p. 17 Kamira/Shutterstock.com; p. 19 Lisa F. Young/Shutterstock. com; p. 20 Kobby Dagan/Shutterstock.com; p. 21 iStockphoto.com/golero; p. 23 possohh/Shutterstock. com; p. 25 Gil.K/Shutterstock.com; p. 27 Arne Hodalic/Corbis Historical/Getty Images; p. 28 Apichartza/Shutterstock.com; p. 29 Gary Hershorn/Corbis Sport/ Getty Images; p. 30 Brothers Good/ Shutterstock.com.

Cataloging-in-Publication Data

Names: Shofner, Melissa Raé.
Title: The people and culture of Cuba / Melissa Raé Shofner.
Description: New York : PowerKids Press, 2018. | Series: Celebrating Hispanic diversity | Includes index.
Identifiers: ISBN 9781538327074 (pbk.) | ISBN 9781508163114 (library bound) | ISBN 9781538327517 (6 pack)
Subjects: LCSH: Cuba–Juvenile literature. | Cuba–Social life and customs–Juvenile literature.
Classification: LCC F1758.5 S56 2018 | DDC 972.91–dc23

Manufactured in the United States of America

CPSIA Compliance Information: Batch #BW18PK: For Further Information contact Rosen Publishing, New York, New York at 1-800-237-9932

CONTENTS

WELCOME TO CUBA

The Republic of Cuba is an island located about 100 miles (160.9 km) south of Key West, Florida. It's about 750 miles (1,207 km) long and is the largest island in the Caribbean Sea, even though it's only about 60 miles (96.6 km) across at its widest point.

Cuba is a Spanish-speaking country. Its **culture** is a bold mix of African, European, and native islander influences, and many Cubans have a Spanish background. The rich **heritage** of Cuba can be seen in the country's food, religion, art, and music.

A country's government often has an effect on its culture. This is especially true in Cuba, a country that has in large part been shaped by its troubled political history.

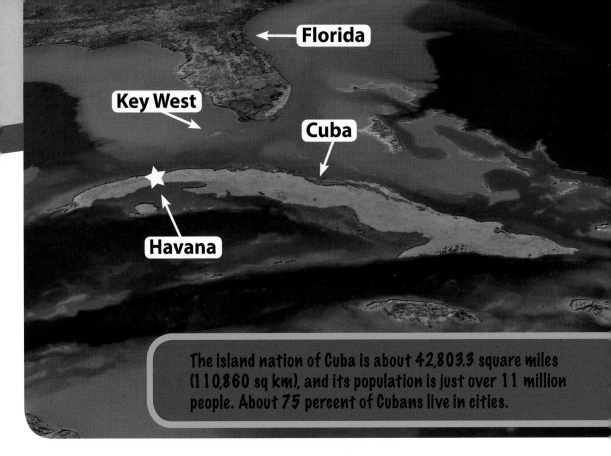

Florida

Key West

Cuba

Havana

The island nation of Cuba is about **42,803.3** square miles (**110,860** sq km), and its population is just over **11** million people. About **75** percent of Cubans live in cities.

Language Is Important

You may have heard people use the term "Hispanic" to describe people when they actually meant to say "Latino." These terms are often confused, but they can't be used **interchangeably**. "Latino" is a term for a person living in the United States whose ancestors are from Latin America. Some people don't use either term to describe themselves. When someone tells you how to talk about their identity, it's important to respect that by using the language they prefer.

NATURAL BEAUTY

Cuba includes about 2,000 small islands that surround the larger main island. When viewed from high above, the main island looks like an alligator. Some people refer to Cuba in Spanish as El Caimán because of its shape.

The landscape of Cuba includes jungles, grasslands, deserts, and forests. However, about 25 percent of the island is covered with hills or mountains, and much of the rest is plains. The island's climate is tropical, or hot and wet. The average annual temperature is about 77° Fahrenheit (25° Celsius). Hurricanes are possible in the area between July and October.

Sugarcane and tobacco plants are Cuba's most important crops. Cuban cigars are famous around the world for their quality. Coffee, fish, and nickel are also important products.

The land in Viñales Valley is perfect for farming. Tobacco has been grown in the valley using traditional methods for hundreds of years.

Natural Resources

Viñales Valley, located at the western end of Cuba, is known for its physical geography as well as its **traditional** culture. Rounded hills called *mogotes* are scattered across the valley. Some stand up to 984.3 feet (300 m) tall. The traditional styles of homes, farming methods, crafts, and music have been preserved in Viñales even though the valley is often visited by outsiders.

9

A TROUBLED HISTORY

Cuba's historical and political background has played a large role in the country's culture. The first groups to live in Cuba were the Guanahatabey and Ciboney peoples. The Taíno people of Venezuela took over the island around 1,000 years ago.

In 1492, Christopher Columbus claimed Cuba for Spain. Spanish settlers began arriving in 1511. They brought African slaves to grow and harvest sugarcane. They also brought warfare and diseases that killed many of the native peoples.

During the Spanish-American War of 1892, the United States helped push Spanish forces out of Cuba. After the war ended, Cuba was given its independence from Spain, but the United States remained involved in the country's affairs. In 1902, the Republic of Cuba was established. Unfortunately, Cuba's new government was weak and many people lived in poverty.

In this image from *Harper's Magazine* (1852), slaves are shown working on a sugarcane plantation in Cuba. The cultures of the Spaniards, Africans, and native peoples had already started to mix by this time.

Fulgencio Batista was a Cuban soldier who became the leader of Cuba from 1933 to 1944. During this time, he created an effective government and made many improvements to the country. Batista lead Cuba again from 1952 until 1959, this time as a dictator. This meant he had total power, which he used to gain money and treat people very badly.

Fidel Castro grew up working in Cuba's sugarcane fields. He later became a lawyer who fought for the rights of poor people. Castro and his brother Raúl were against Batista, and they fought alongside others to overthrow him. Batista left Cuba in 1959, and Castro took control of the country, setting up a system of communism. Some Cubans hoped communism would end their hardships, while others were opposed to it.

This painting of Fidel Castro hangs in the National Museum of Fine Arts in the capital city of Havana, Cuba. Although he was often considered a dictator, Castro was also a symbol of revolution around the world.

What Is Communism?

Communism is a type of government and an economic system in which goods are owned publicly rather than privately. In an ideal communist system, people work to their abilities and receive goods according to their needs. This is different from capitalism, which is a system in which a country's goods and trade are controlled by private owners rather than the state. Communist countries rose to power in the early 1900s during the two World Wars. Today, Cuba, China, North Korea, Laos, and Vietnam are the only communist countries that remain.

A SHIFT IN POWER

At first, other communist countries such as the Soviet Union supported Cuba. The United States, however, was against communism and stopped trading with Cuba. In 1962, the United States threatened Cuba after discovering Soviet **missiles** there. Eventually, the Soviet Union agreed to remove the missiles from Cuba. Cuba lost a valuable **ally** when the Soviet Union collapsed in 1991.

Fidel Castro served as the prime minister, president, and commander of the armed forces of Cuba for nearly 50 years. In 2008, health issues caused him to step down and hand power over to his brother Raúl.

In 2008, relations between Cuba and the United States started to improve. In 2015, the United States reopened its Cuban **embassy** for the first time in over 50 years. Cuba soon did the same with its embassy in the United States.

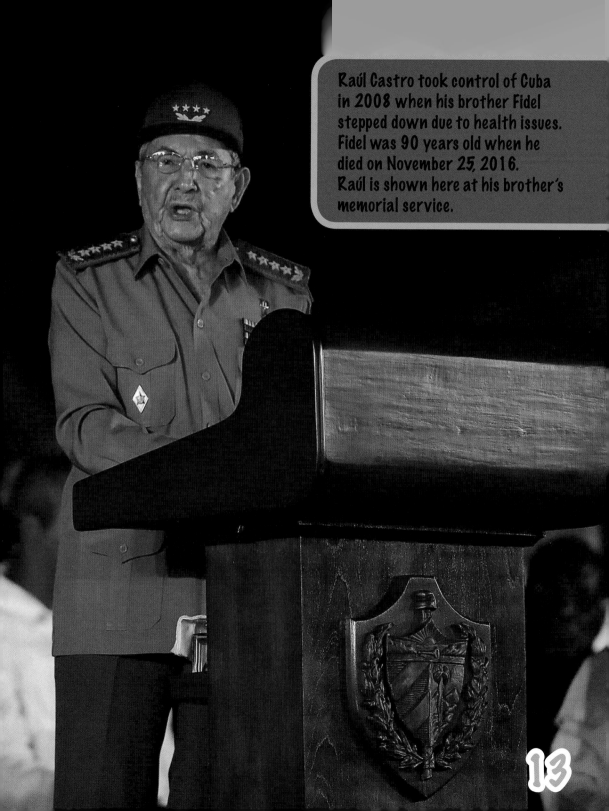

Raúl Castro took control of Cuba in 2008 when his brother Fidel stepped down due to health issues. Fidel was 90 years old when he died on November 25, 2016. Raúl is shown here at his brother's memorial service.

13

GOVERNMENT INFLUENCE

The culture of Cuba is different from that of many other Hispanic countries. It greatly reflects its historical connection to Spain, but it also features a great deal of African influence, which can be seen in the country's dancing, art, and music.

Before 1959, Cuba's largest cities served as the cultural centers of the country. After the 1959 revolution, however, Castro's new government worked hard to bring the country's culture to Cubans across the island. A government agency, or organization, called the Ministry of Culture was set up in 1976 to spread Cuban culture. The Ministry of Culture helped establish more than 200 museums and around 2,000 libraries in Cuba. Cubans were also given greater access to music, theater, art, and dance lessons.

Education is important to the people of Cuba. Schools are free and run by the government. Children are required by law to attend, and they learn about communism from an early age.

Religion in Cuba

Before the revolution, much of the Cuban population identified as Roman Catholic, though few people practiced the religion. Under Castro, more than 400 Catholic schools were closed. The Communist Party lifted its ban on religion in 1991. Today, Santeria, a West African religion, is practiced by many and is an important part of Cuban culture.

NATIONAL HOLIDAYS

On July 26, 1953, Castro and a group of **rebels** attacked the Moncada army base in Santiago de Cuba. This was the first serious strike against Batista's dictatorship by a rebel group, and it started the revolution. The attack failed, but it symbolized the desire of many Cubans to overthrow Batista.

Cuba has celebrated National Revolution Day on July 26 since 1959. Since 1976, July 25 and 27 have also been included. During the three-day National Revolution Day celebration, schools and businesses close, the revolution flag is flown, and speeches and rallies are held throughout the country. National Revolution Day is possibly Cuba's most important holiday.

October 10 is Cuba's Independence Day celebration. On this date in 1868, Cuba began to fight for freedom from Spain, which was achieved in 1902.

Carnival is held in Santiago de Cuba and Havana each year in late July, often around the time of the National Revolution Day celebration. Carnival is a colorful 10-day event filled with music and dancing. It celebrates Cuba's mix of Spanish and African cultures.

Christmas Returns to Cuba

In 1969, the Cuban government declared that Christmas was no longer a national holiday. This was during a time when the government was viewed as antireligious because it believed churches were against the revolution. Many religious leaders left or were removed from the country around that time. Christmas was made a national holiday again in 1997, just before Pope John Paul II's visit to Cuba in 1998.

SIMPLE CUISINE

Cuban meals are often simple. Many dishes include rice and beans. *Criollo* is a cooking style used in many Hispanic countries, including Cuba and Puerto Rico. *Criollo* cooking mixes meat—such as chicken, beef, or pork—with rice, beans, a variety of vegetables, and spices. Sandwiches, soups, and stews are also popular dishes.

A sauce called *sofrito* is made using a tomato base. Garlic, peppers, and fresh tomatoes are added along with a bit of flour. This makes *sofrito* a tasty addition to many Cuban meals.

Due to government rules and limits on trade, food in Cuba is rationed. This means it's handed out by the government in fixed amounts. Certain foods, such as meats, are sometimes hard to find. Most restaurants in Cuba are also run by the government.

Many Cuban dishes include rice and beans, vegetables, and fried plantains. Plantains are similar to bananas. Meat is included in meals when it's available.

19

CASUAL CLOTHING

Today, the people of Cuba mostly wear modern Western clothing. Men often wear comfortable pants or shorts with a loose-fitting top or T-shirt. Women often wear skirts or dresses.

These women are wearing traditional rumba-style dresses.

GUAYABERA

Traditional Cuban fashion is a blend of Spanish and African styles. A strong Latin influence is seen in the puffy sleeves, layered skirts, and bright tops with embroidery, or stitched designs. African styles, such as headwraps, are often worn. Rumba dresses, named for a style of Cuban music and dance, are brightly colored with many ruffles. Today, rumba-style dresses are worn for special occasions, such as celebrations and weddings, or for tourist events.

Cuban men traditionally wore a guayabera shirt, which has two or four pockets and folds of fabric called pleats down the front and back. These shirts are still popular today.

EXPLORING THE ARTS

The Cuban government supports the arts, which feature a mix of styles due to the country's blended heritage. In the past, art was **censored** by the government. Today, the growing popularity of Cuban art in other areas, including the United States and Europe, is bringing money into Cuba. This has lead the government to loosen its **restrictions** and even send Cuban art out to exhibits around the world.

Today, more than 200 neighborhood cultural centers, or *casas de culturas*, are found throughout Cuba. They offer workshops for people who are interested in all types of art. The Cuban government encourages talented artists and has set up the Cuban Film Institute, the National School for the Arts, and the National Cultural Council as ways to support them.

Pictured here is the Gran Teatro de Havana. Old American cars, such as the ones parked here, may be seen all over Cuba.

Cuban Cinema

Each year, Cuba hosts the New Latin American Film Festival, which is also called the Havana Film Festival. Film has been a big industry in Cuba since the revolution of 1959. Many people in Cuba enjoy going to the cinema, or movie theater. Movie tickets only cost about 14 cents because the government controls film production.

23

MUSIC IN THE STREETS

Music is very important to the people of Cuba. Both traditional and modern music styles take advantage of the rich Spanish and African cultural heritage of the country. Afro-Cuban music has become a symbol of national identity. Music is also a big part of the Santeria religion. Santeria plays a large role in the culture of Cuba.

There are a number of musical styles in Cuba, including son and rumba. Son music features something called the **anticipated** bass, which is a low note before the downbeat in a song. Son music often has themes of patriotism and love. Rumba is a popular, upbeat style of music that people often dance to. "Rumba" may come from the verb *rumbear*, which means something like "to party" or "to have a good time."

Cubans love to play music. They can often be found performing on the street or in their homes.

Alicia Alonso

One of Cuba's most well-known dancers is Alicia Alonso, a ballerina of international fame. Alonso was born in Havana on December 21, 1921, and is best known for her roles in the ballets *Carmen Suite* and *Giselle*. She danced with ballet companies around the world, but later returned to Cuba to start the Ballet Nacional de Cuba.

25

CUBAN LITERATURE

After the revolution, literature in Cuba faced censorship. In 1987, however, the government lightened its restrictions. Today, important ideas may be openly shared as long as they don't go against the country.

Many types of literature are popular in Cuba, including novels, short stories, and poetry. There are several Cuban literary magazines, too. José Martí (1853–1895) was a poet who promoted Cuban freedom in his writings. His work inspired others to write about winning independence. Nicolás Guillén (1902–1989), an **activist** poet, was the national poet of Cuba. He played a large role in the creation of Afro-Cuban literature.

Ernest Hemingway (1899–1961) was an American writer who lived in Cuba for many years. His novels *Islands in the Stream* and *The Old Man and the Sea* are set in Cuba.

Hemingway and Fidel Castro met one day at a fishing tournament.

PLAY BALL!

In Cuba, a government agency called the National Institute of Sports, Physical Education, and Recreation is in charge of many of the country's sports and recreational activities. Sports are very important to the people of Cuba, and the program gives citizens the opportunity to take part in their favorite activities.

Most Hispanic countries favor soccer over all other sports. However, in Cuba, the national sport is baseball. The United States introduced Cuba to the sport of baseball in the 1860s. Since that time, many star players have come out of Cuba.

The people of Cuba also enjoy basketball, soccer, and volleyball. Boxing is a popular sport, and many Olympic champions have come from Cuba. Cubans also love to play dominoes, a tile-matching game.

On July 12, 2015, Cuba played baseball against the United States at the Pan-American Games in Toronto, Canada. Cuba's national baseball team is one of the greatest in the world.

SHARING CUBAN CULTURE

When Fidel Castro rose to power in 1959, a large number of wealthy Cubans left the country. Many of these people went to Miami, the second-largest city in Florida.

Today, Miami is a busy city with a strong Cuban presence and influence. The neighborhood of Little Havana is a center of Hispanic culture and features the sights, sounds, and flavors of Cuba throughout its streets. Viernes Culturales, or Cultural Fridays, are held in Little Havana on the last Friday of each month to celebrate the Hispanic and Cuban culture of the neighborhood.

Sharing Cuban culture with the world is sometimes difficult due to government restrictions, especially when it comes to the United States. Hopefully, relations between Cuba and the United States will continue to improve.

GLOSSARY

activist: Someone who acts strongly in support of or against an issue.

ally: A person or country associated with another for a common purpose.

anticipate: To think about in advance.

censor: To change or cut parts of something or ban something entirely after examining it.

culture: The beliefs and ways of life of a certain group of people.

embassy: The residence or offices of an official representative of a country in another country.

heritage: The traditions and beliefs that are part of the history of a group or nation.

interchangeable: The ability of two or more things to be put in the place of one another.

missile: An object that is shot or launched to strike something from a distance.

rebel: Someone who fights against authority.

restriction: Something that limits or controls.

traditional: Following what's been done for a long time.

INDEX

WEBSITES

Due to the changing nature of Internet links, PowerKids Press has developed an online list of websites related to the subject of this book. This site is updated regularly. Please use this link to access the list: www.powerkidslinks.com/chd/cuba